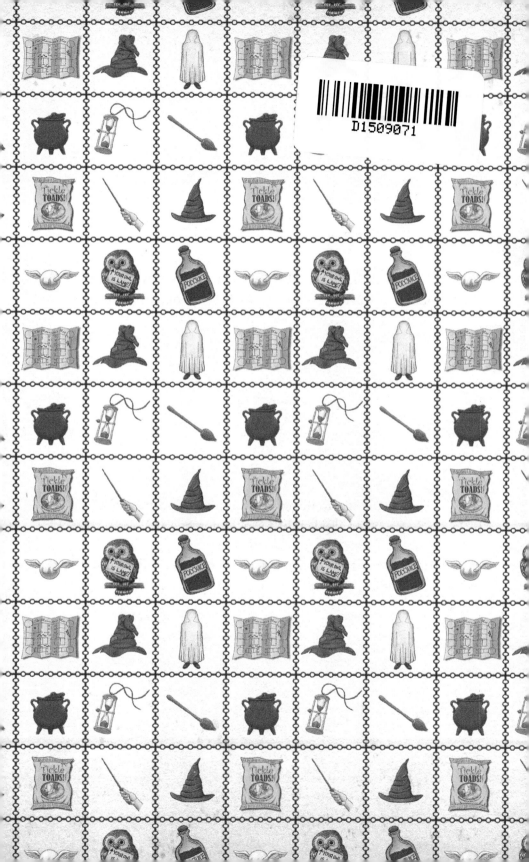

This book is dedicated to all the witches and wizards out there —
regardless of whether they've received their Hogwarts letters yet.

Birdy would like to thank her wonderful husband, Adrian,
and also her little Gryffindor, Stellan.

Laura would like to thank her husband, Cody, the greatest
Hufflepuff of all time. (Sorry, Cedric Diggory.)

THE UNOFFICIAL

HARRY POTTER
INSULTS HANDBOOK

101 COMEBACKS
FOR THE WICKED WIZARDS
AND WITCHES IN YOUR LIFE

BIRDY JONES & LAURA J. MOSS

ILLUSTRATIONS BY STERLING MARTIN

TESTIMONIALS

"This book gave me the confidence to stand up for myself. Now if only they'd make a book that would teach me how to pull my wand out of my nose."
-BRYAN BIGGLES, HUFFLEPUFF

"I used to spend every afternoon crying in the bathroom with Moaning Myrtle, but things changed after I armed myself with these insults. I haven't been bullied in over a year! This is the best book in the world!*"
-MRS. H. PERBOLEE, HUFFLEPUFF

"Peeves stole this book from me while I was in Potions class. Now he's worse than ever."
-YOLANDA PERKINS, RAVENCLAW

"This handbook would really help my brother who gets wedgies every day. After I read it a few more times, maybe I'll pass it along to him."
-SANDY SPROUTSWORTH, RAVENCLAW

"Before this guide, I was the butt of every Slytherin joke. But after reading it, I feel like a true Gryffindor!"
-NEVILLE LONGBOTTOM, GRYFFINDOR

"This book has ruined my life. I've got no one left to pick on, so I've had to take up Gobstones."
-KEVIN CURDS, SLYTHERIN

* *This statement has not been verified by the Ministry of Magic.*

INTRODUCTION

Are you tormented in Transfiguration?

Are you mocked for your Muggle mum?

Do you long for a Time-Turner so you can always deliver a killer comeback?

Whether you're a N.E.W.T.-level wizard or a wide-eyed witch still awaiting your Hogwarts acceptance letter, you've probably encountered a merciless Malfoy or despicable Dursley who makes your magical blood boil. If you've ever stood speechless as someone called you a talentless squib, a worthless git or a filthy mudblood, this is the book for you!

Study these magical pages closely and with a little Hufflepuff hard work, you'll soon brave any bully with the courage of a Gryffindor and be able to outwit even the smartest Ravenclaw or the most cunning Slytherin!

REPEAT
AFTER ME...

I SOLEMNLY SWEAR TO USE THIS BOOK FOR GOOD

HISTORY OF THE MAGICAL BULLY

Bullies have existed in the magical world for as long as magic itself has been around. Indeed, even young witches and wizards of prehistoric times had to contend with magical menaces who transfigured innocent witches into woolly mammoths and used their wands to aim wind up the loincloths of unsuspecting wizards.

However, it wasn't until the year 1000 A.D. that we find our first well-documented case of a wizard bully — none other than Salazar Slytherin himself. It was around this time that Slytherin and three other great witches and wizards of the age — Godric Gryffindor, Helga Hufflepuff and Rowena Ravenclaw — decided to form Hogwarts School of Witchcraft and Wizardry. Disagreements over what kind of students should be allowed to study at the school are what led to some of the first instances of magical bullying.

It all started when Slytherin, tired of Hufflepuff's never-ending attempts to mediate the foursome's disagreements, performed a Switching Spell and replaced Hufflepuff's sugar with salt. Naturally, this little prank resulted in a very bad cup of tea — and Gryffindor's using a Hurling Hex to throw the tea into Slytherin's face. At this point, Ravenclaw intervened and suggested that Hogwarts admit only those students with the greatest intellectual potential, so Slytherin silenced her with a wave of his wand and told her that her diadem made her look fat. From this point on, Slytherin became a relentless bully — calling his colleagues names, cursing them whenever they turned their backs and repeatedly threatening them with the monster he claimed to have hidden in Hogwarts.

The Mirror of Erised and Hogwarts' Wi-Fi router. (location unknown)

Perhaps the next most famous incidents of magical bullying occurred in 1689 immediately following the signing of the International Statute of Wizarding Secrecy. Ironically, the statute was introduced to end the widespread persecution of wizarding children by Muggles, but resulted in extensive Muggle-baiting and bullying. In fact, according to ancient wizarding texts, the first recorded instance of a shrinking key occurred just a year later in 1690.

As you know, bullies still walk the halls of magical education institutions from the icy mountains surrounding Durmstrang to the balmy beaches outside Beauxbatons. And, of course, Hogwarts has its share of bullies too. While Slytherin House continues to produce the greatest number of belligerent bullies — namely, the terrible You-Know-Who — they're not exclusive to this house. Ravenclaw has been known to house a number of hostile know-it-alls, a handful of Gryffindors have used their courage for less-than-honorable means, and even Hufflepuff has produced a not-so-friendly witch. Indeed, even some of those wizards we hold in high regard today — including Harry Potter's own godfather, Sirius Black — had a sordid history of bullying in their past. It's no surprise then that Albus Dumbledore decreed there would be no Wi-Fi at Hogwarts and hid the school's router. After all, when young witches and wizards are already armed with curses and hexes, the last thing they need is access to social media.

WORKS CITED

Bagshot, Bathilda. A History of Magic. 1st edition. London Little Red Books. 1947.

QUIT HITTING YOURSELF

The halls of Hogwarts can be intimidating for even the most courageous of Gryffindors. A student's education in the wonders of wizardry is filled with perils — from advanced Potions to Defense Against the Dark Arts — and every legendary wizard has confronted a dreaded wand-yielding roughneck. Harry Potter battled He-Who-Must-Not-Be-Named, the greatest magical bully of our time — and that's not all. Harry faced other rude ruffians, including Acromantulas, Whomping Willows, Malfoys, basilisks, Lestranges, trolls and horcruxes, just to name a few. And while Harry sometimes felt he wasn't good enough to take on all these magical menaces, he pulled himself up by his robe-straps and found the confidence he needed to defeat some of the worst bullies ever. Even Ron Weasley, Harry's skittish best friend, was able to summon Gryffindor's courage to vanquish his worst enemies. So don't worry! This handbook is here to help you become a confident, fearless wizard who can dish out the snappiest insults to the worst of Hogwarts' hooligans. Quit hitting yourself! You're going to be a great wizard. Just wait and see...

Still doubting yourself? Don't! Believe it or not, some of the most celebrated sorcerers in history were also the victims of belligerent bullies! Keep an eye out for Famous Wizard Insults cards to learn more about these historically humiliated witches and wizards.

WAYS TO IDENTIFY A MAGICAL BULLY

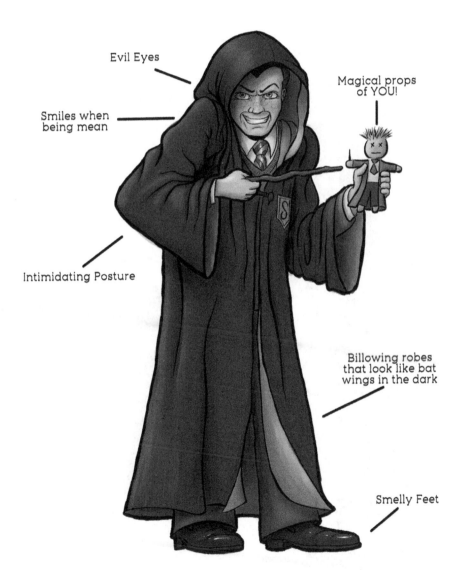

Evil Eyes

Smiles when being mean

Magical props of YOU!

Intimidating Posture

Billowing robes that look like bat wings in the dark

Smelly Feet

TIPS FOR A SUCCESSFUL DELIVERY

These diagrams will show you the correct and incorrect ways to execute a cutting comeback. If you follow the advice on these drawings, you'll have great success at delivering magical insults!

THE WRONG WAY

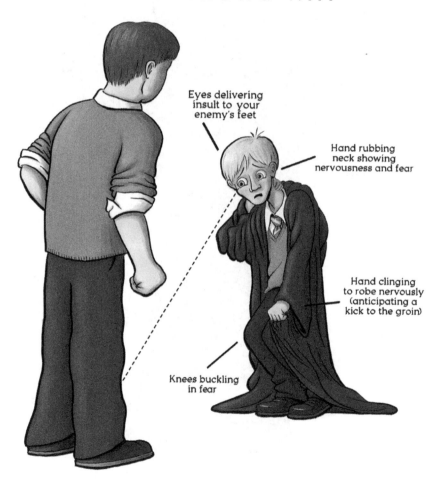

Eyes delivering insult to your enemy's feet

Hand rubbing neck showing nervousness and fear

Hand clinging to robe nervously (anticipating a kick to the groin)

Knees buckling in fear

THE RIGHT WAY

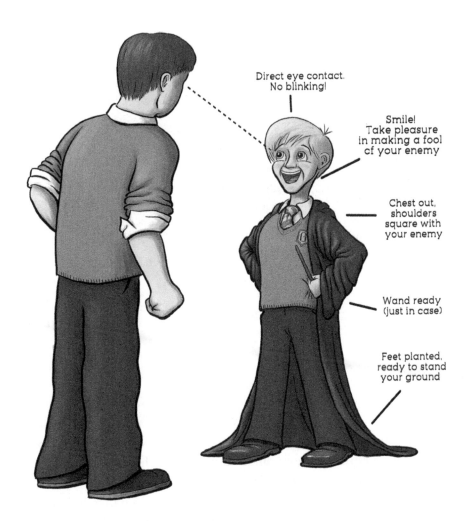

Direct eye contact.
No blinking!

Smile!
Take pleasure
in making a fool
of your enemy

Chest out,
shoulders
square with
your enemy

Wand ready
(just in case)

Feet planted,
ready to stand
your ground

See the difference?
Confidence really goes a long way.

A TEST TO BEGIN ALL TESTS

Before you begin your education in magical insults, take this quiz to assess whether you're a Spineless Sorcerer, a Wand-Happy Wizard or something in between.

1. You're walking to Herbology when the class bully sticks out his foot and trips you. Do you...

a. Burst into tears and bury your face in the mud.

b. Consider cursing him but think better of it.

c. Start throwing punches — you're going to settle this with a Muggle duel!

2. The girl who's been tormenting you since you were a first-year is spreading a rumor that you're half troll. Do you...

a. Try to ignore your classmates' whispers and giggles but cry yourself to sleep.

b. Report her to a teacher.

c. Lock her in the bathroom with a full-grown mountain troll.

3. You're eating Pumpkin Pasties when a sneaky Slytherin performs a Switching Spell and suddenly there's a rat spleen in your mouth. Do you...

a. Continue chewing and pretend you don't notice.

b. Spit it out and give that Slytherin your meanest glare.

c. Hex him until Professor McGonagall pries the wand from your fingers.

HOW DID YOU SCORE?

Spineless Sorcerer (mostly A's)
You're getting kicked around like a house-elf without a backbone. Wipe away those tears, grab a quill and start taking notes because you're about to get schooled in how to combat magical bullies.

Wishy-Washy Warlock (mostly B's)
You want to stick up for yourself but lack confidence. Get a few snappy comebacks under your belt and with a little bit of practice, you'll be telling off bullies before you know it!

Wand-Happy Wizard (mostly C's)
Whoa! Put down your fists, step away from your wand and take a deep breath. You need to learn how to deal with a bully in ways that won't land you in detention.

THE CHOSEN ONE

This book presents itself only to those who are truly worthy, so the mere fact that you're holding it in your hands right now means that you are pure of heart, strong of character and ready to put those magical bullies in their place. In other words, you are The Chosen One, little wizard, so get ready to spit comebacks like a Hungarian Horntail spits fire!

As you work your way through this handbook, make note of your favorite insults, commit them to memory and practice your delivery so you'll be ready when it comes time to use them. To help you prepare, you'll encounter R.A.T.s (Real-life Application Tests) throughout this book, which will test your magical wits and challenge you to think on your feet.

Also, keep in mind that these comebacks are powerful tools that must be wielded with caution. So first, a few words of wisdom:

1. Be careful when using these insults on younger siblings because your parents just may send you a mortifying Howler right in the middle of breakfast. (Remember the last time that happened? Your ears were ringing with your mother's shrieks for days.)
2. If a bully is relentless or ever physically harms you, put the wand — and the insults! — away and tell a grown-up witch or wizard. (Preferably an intimidating one like Professor McGonagall because no one is going to mess with her.)
3. Be wary of becoming a bully yourself. It's one thing to ward off a bully with your wit, but it's another thing entirely to transform from the bullied to the bully. (That's not the kind of Switching Spell we can get behind.)

And now, turn the page, Chosen One, because it's time for your education in magical comebacks to begin!

ACCIO INSULTS!

YOU'RE SO UGLY VOLDEMORT
WON'T SPEAK YOUR NAME.

EVERY TIME YOU SPEAK IT FEELS LIKE
YOU'VE CAST CRUCIO ON ME.

AVADA KEDAVRA DIDN'T KILL
DUMBLEDORE — YOUR BREATH DID.

YOU AND HARRY HAVE SOMETHING
IN COMMON: YOU BOTH SPEND YOUR
BIRTHDAYS ALONE.

I WISH PROTEGO COULD SHIELD ME
FROM YOUR EXISTENCE.

DOES HAGRID KNOW YOU'RE OUT OF YOUR CAGE?

HERE'S SOME FLOO POWDER. BE SURE TO SPEAK UNINTELLIGIBLY.

GO INTO THE ROOM OF REQUIREMENT AND DISAPPEAR LIKE ROWENA'S DIADEM.

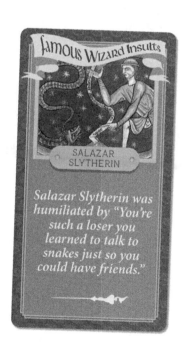

Famous Wizard Insults

SALAZAR SLYTHERIN

Salazar Slytherin was humiliated by "You're such a loser you learned to talk to snakes just so you could have friends."

YOU'RE SO DUMB YOU THOUGHT QUAFFLES NEEDED SYRUP.

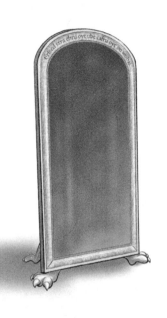

YOU'RE THE FOURTH UNFORGIVABLE CURSE.

WHEN YOU ENCOUNTER A BOGGART, DOES IT TURN INTO A MIRROR?

YOU KEEP TALKING, BUT ALL I HEAR IS MOANING MYRTLE.

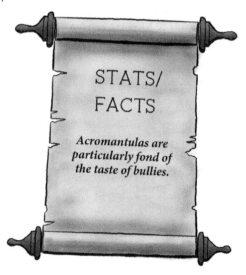

STATS/ FACTS

Acromantulas are particularly fond of the taste of bullies.

FOLLOW THE SPIDERS. SERIOUSLY.

THE OGRE

Because he's notoriously slow, you'll have time to shout two or three insults before he starts throwing punches. Run fast and don't let him catch you, or you'll get a noogie that will hurt for days.

PRACTICAL JOKE

Dealing with a total know-it-all? Mix up a Confusion Concoction and slip her some before O.W.L.s.

I ASKED SNAPE HOW LONG YOU'VE BEEN INSUFFERABLE. HE SAID "ALWAYS."

YEAH, YOUR BLOOD IS PURE. PURELY AWFUL.

I'D LIKE TO TURN ALL YOUR BELONGINGS INTO PORTKEYS.

OWLS DELIVERED HARRY'S ACCEPTANCE LETTER. REGRET DELIVERED YOURS.

I'D SEND YOU TO
AZKABAN, BUT THAT
WOULD BE UNFAIR
TO THE PRISONERS.

YOU'RE SO HORRIBLE YOUR PATRONUS
IS DOLORES UMBRIDGE.

I CAN TELL YOU
DIDN'T GET
AN O.W.L. IN
TRANSFIGURATION.
OTHERWISE, YOU
WOULD'VE DONE
SOMETHING ABOUT
YOUR FACE.

WARNING

*Use these insults
on Snape at
your own risk.*

I'D SAY THAT I LIKE YOU, BUT I SHALL NOT TELL LIES.

LEAVE BEFORE I DO SOMETHING THAT ALLOWS ME TO SEE A THESTRAL.

YOU SUCK THE LIFE OUT OF A PARTY LIKE A DEMENTOR SUCKS THE SOUL OUT OF A MOUTH.

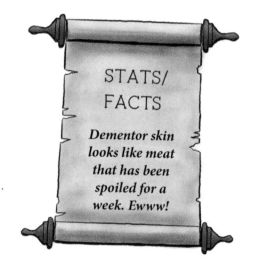

STATS/ FACTS

Dementor skin looks like meat that has been spoiled for a week. Ewww!

LET'S MAKE AN UNBREAKABLE VOW
THAT YOU NEVER COME NEAR ME.

WHENEVER SOMEONE SAYS SOMETHING
NICE ABOUT YOU, MY SNEAKOSCOPE
STARTS WHISTLING.

WHEN I WALK PAST THE ROOM OF
REQUIREMENT, I IMAGINE A ROOM
WITHOUT YOU IN IT.

I THOUGHT $9^{3/4}$ WAS YOUR IQ.

DID YOU KNOW?

You can require a room where there are no bullies to be found.

R.A.T.s POP QUIZ
(REAL-LIFE APPLICATION TEST)

TEST 1: BANISHING THE BAD-MOUTHED BULLY

It's a beautiful day in Hogsmeade. Crimson leaves drift down from the trees and nestle on the thatched roofs of cottages and shops, and there's a slight chill to the air, announcing the arrival of autumn and the evening's Halloween Feast at Hogwarts. You enter Honeyduke's, debating whether to buy a Fizzing Whizbee or a Jelly Slug, when you notice a group of your classmates whispering and pointing in your direction. You glance over your shoulder and don't see anyone else. Yep, they're definitely talking about you.

The class bully saunters up to you, a sneer across his pinched face, and says, "I was just telling everyone that you don't need to wear a mask for Halloween. Your face is scary enough."

Your cheeks grow warm and your classmates' giggles echo in your ears, but you simply take a deep breath, shrug your shoulders and…

a. Hurl a Peppermint Toad at his head.

b. Say "When you encounter a Boggart, does it turn into a mirror?"

c. Run away and vow never to set foot in Hogsmeade again.

d. Hiss some indiscernible words and hope a venomous snake appears to do your bidding.

Correct Answer: b

TOOLS OF THE MAGICAL TRADE

Sometimes a wizard needs a little help when trying to avoid a magical bully. The following list of tools will come in handy when you need to make it to class wedgie-free!

A WAND

A good wizard's last line of defense. Armed with this book, it's rare that you'll have to use it.

MARAUDER'S MAP

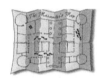

This is handy when avoiding bullying hotspots such as behind the Herbology greenhouses or underneath the Quidditch bleachers.

INVISIBILITY CLOAK

Because this is extremely rare and valuable, we recommend arming yourself with insults from this book instead.

POLYJUICE POTION

When bullies are looking for you, sometimes the safest way to make it to your classes is to change into someone else!

TIME-TURNER

Repair your reputation by traveling back in time to deliver that killer comeback!

FAMOUS BULLIES AND THE INSULTS THAT UNDID THEM

As you know, bullies have been around for as long as magic itself, and if you've been reading the Famous Wizard Insults cards scattered throughout these pages, then you're well aware that some of the greatest magical minds in history were the victims of painful pranks and humiliating hexes. But these witches and wizards aren't the only celebrity sorcerers who were tormented by bullies.

For instance, did you know...

★ That Merlin wore that pointed hat to protect himself from swirlies?

★ That Wendelin the Weird got so sick of hearing "your mum's so fat" jokes that she tried to be burned at the stake 47 times?

★ That Agrippa was the first person — wizard or Muggle — to receive a wedgie? (He quit wearing underwear with his toga after that.)

★ That Dumbledore first broke his nose as a third-year when a Slytherin punched him for being a "Muggle sympathizer"?

It's all true!

*Keep reading those Famous Wizard Insults cards for more fascinating facts about magical bullying through the ages.

YOU'RE THE REASON MANDRAKES CRY.

IF VOLDEMORT WERE STILL AROUND, I'D TELL HIM YOU'RE THE CHOSEN ONE.

I SHOULD'VE TAKEN SOME FELIX FELICIS THIS MORNING. THEN MAYBE I WOULDN'T HAVE SEEN YOU TODAY.

AREN'T YOU ON THE COVER OF "THE MONSTER BOOK OF MONSTERS"?

I'D PUSH YOU INTO THE CABINET AT
BORGIN AND BURKES IF I KNEW YOU
WOULDN'T END UP BACK AT HOGWARTS.

DID YOU KNOW?

The mistreatment of House-elves is a form of bullying. Join S.P.E.W. to make a difference!

WHO DRESSED YOU
THIS MORNING?
A HOUSE-ELF?

YOU DON'T EVER
HAVE TO WORRY
ABOUT SOMEONE
SLIPPING YOU A
LOVE POTION.

PRACTICAL JOKE

Whip up a love potion for your nemesis and pour it into Millicent Bulstrode's pumpkin juice.

LUCIUS WAS RIGHT.
DUMBLEDORE WILL
LET ANYONE
IN HERE.

YOUR BREATH IS SO
BAD A DEMENTOR
WOULDN'T
KISS YOU.

UNLESS THE
PROPHECY SAYS
YOU'RE GOING TO
WALK AWAY RIGHT
NOW, I DON'T WANT
TO HEAR IT.

WARNING

Turning into
Crabbe or Goyle
may leave a really
bad stench
on you.

HERE'S SOME
POLYJUICE POTION.
GO TURN INTO
SOMEONE ELSE.

TRICKS AND TREATS FOR MAGICAL BULLIES

KEEP THESE SPECTACULAR SPELLS UP YOUR SLEEVE.

Some of the silliest and most effective anti-bullying spells were created and cast by once-bullied witches and wizards. Check out some of their infamous spellwork below.

Blowsarious: Makes snot bubbles fly out of a bully's nose in weird shapes

Gasplozio: Uncontrollable, putrid smells will escape from a bully's hindquarters

Warto Conflagro: Makes burning warts temporarily form all over a bully's face

Gibberfy: Garbles a bully's words for a full class period

Belcho Escapo: Every time a bully tries to speak, a loud burp comes out instead

SERVE UP SOME SNEAKY SNACKS.

Does your bully have a penchant for picking on you, as well as a taste for sweets? Then visit Dragon & Serpent's Magical Bakery in Diagon Alley and get some of their fresh-baked Bully-B-Gone Treats. One bite of these confectioner's concoctions and your bully will get his or her just desserts.

Snore S'mores: That big-time bully will be sawing logs during class in no time! (And you know McGonagall doesn't take kindly to her students catching Z's in Transfiguration.)

Tickle Toads: Eat these frog-shaped jellies and feel the tickles start in your armpits and feet! *Caution: Laughing for hours will cause side pains and neck strains.*

Smudge Fudge: This trickster fudge makes wiping after a Number Two impossible! *Tip: Consume a small amount of Weasleys' Wizarding Wheezes' U-No-Poo if you accidentally ingest some of this delicious fudge yourself.*

Belly Bickers: Ever heard your stomach growl? Well, this changes your stomach's growls into a full-blown argument that the entire Great Hall will hear.

YOUR PERSONALITY IS WORSE THAN ALL SEVEN HORCRUXES.

SNAPE SENT AN OWL. HE WANTS HIS GREASY HAIR BACK.

SOMETIMES I SYMPATHIZE WITH SIRIUS' MOTHER. I'D WANT TO BLAST YOU OFF MY FAMILY TREE TOO.

YOU'RE SO UGLY HOGWARTS WAS NAMED AFTER YOU.

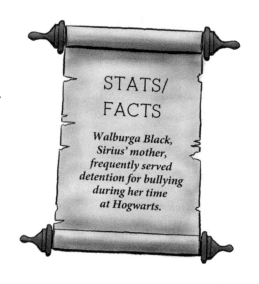

STATS/ FACTS

Walburga Black, Sirius' mother, frequently served detention for bullying during her time at Hogwarts.

THE MEATHEAD

He's as strong as a full-grown mountain troll and just as terrifying. Sling insults at him to confuse him, but be sure to run away before he starts swinging his Beater's Bat at your face!

DID YOU KNOW?

Fred Weasley is rumored to have made up this insult about Cornelius Fudge.

YOU'RE SO DUMB YOU TRIED TO EAT CORNELIUS FUDGE.

YOU'RE THE REASON THERE'S A BAN ON EXPERIMENTAL BREEDING.

YOU'RE SO DUMB THAT CONFUNDO MAKES YOU SEEM SMARTER.

I'VE MET FLOBBERWORMS MORE INTERESTING THAN YOU.

HOW YOU BECAME A WIZARD IS ONE FOR THE DEPARTMENT OF MYSTERIES.

WHEN I LOOK INTO THE MIRROR OF ERISED, EVERYTHING IS THE SAME— YOU'RE JUST NOT THERE.

YOU'RE SO DUMB YOU JOINED THE DEATH EATERS BECAUSE YOU WERE HUNGRY.

IF YOU HAD A PHOENIX, IT WOULDN'T BOTHER WITH REBIRTH.

STATS/ FACTS

Phoenixes never insult people, but they will occasionally let droppings land on bullies' heads.

GO INSULT A
HIPPOGRIFF.

YOUR FACE HAS
THE SAME EFFECT
ON ME AS A PUKING
PASTILLE.

WARNING

*NEVER insult a
hippogriff unless
you want a
talon to the face.*

OLLIVANDER GAVE
YOU A WAND
TO MATCH YOUR
HEAD: THICK
AND HOLLOW.

YOUR BUTT IS AS
EXPLOSIVE
AS A BLAST-ENDED
SKREWT.

A LITTLE CHEEK CAN HAVE CONSEQUENCES

Sometimes witches and wizards will resort to physical forms of Muggle bullying — and we don't just mean casting a pesky Trip Jinx. Below, you'll find a few scenarios to prepare for in case your bully responds to your killer comebacks with muscle.

THE ARM BURN

THE NOOGIE

THE SWIRLIE

THE MAGIC CARPET RIDE

THE WEDGIE

QUIT HITTING YOURSELF

What do you do if a bully actually hurts you? As awesome as it was when Hermione slapped Draco during their third year, it's best to avoid a physical confrontation like this. Instead, report the incident to a trusted grown-up witch or wizard and let them handle it. As Dumbledore said, "Help will always be given at Hogwarts to those who ask for it."

(Extra Tip: We suggest going to Hagrid. After all, wouldn't your bully look nice with a pigtail coming out of his backside?)

I ALSO GRAB MY FOREHEAD IN PAIN
WHEN I THINK OF YOU.

NO ONE BOTHERS
FOLLOWING
YOU ON THE
MARAUDER'S MAP.

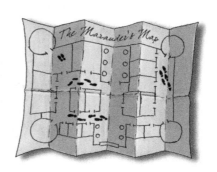

YOU'RE SO UGLY THE MINISTRY OF
MAGIC THOUGHT YOU WERE AN
UNREGISTERED ANIMAGUS.

PRACTICAL JOKE

Disguise yourself as a
Ministry of Magic official
and ask your bully to fill out
an Animagus Registry
form.

I'D PLAY BEATER
IF YOU WERE THE
BLUDGER.

R.A.T.s POP QUIZ

(REAL-LIFE APPLICATION TEST)

TEST 2: QUICK COMEBACKS ON THE QUIDDITCH PITCH

You've spent the summer practicing Quidditch with your brother's hand-me-down broom and a bewitched golf ball, dodging imaginary Bludgers and catching that tiny ball every single time. You've even perfected the troublesome Wronski Feint, which, more often than not, resulted in a bloody nose. But the long hours of training and countless bloody handkerchiefs have paid off: You're the new Seeker on the House team — the youngest in nearly a century!

Now, the day of truth has finally arrived. It's the first Quidditch match of the season and your insides are writhing. (You feel rather like you've swallowed a couple of Cockroach Clusters and a handful of Gillyweed.) As you step onto the Quidditch pitch, you hear the cheers and jeers from your classmates, and then the opposing team's Seeker jabs you with his shoulder and knocks you to the ground. (Honestly, isn't he a little big to be playing Seeker?)

"I'd hate to see who else tried out for Seeker if you're the best your team has to offer," the brute sneers. Luckily, you're prepared for this. You square your shoulders, look that bully in the eye and...

a. Burst into tears and join Moaning Myrtle in the U-bend.

b. Say nothing and hope you'll catch the Snitch before he does.

c. Report him to Madam Hooch for teasing you.

d. Say "Well, I'd play Beater if you were the Bludger."

Correct Answer: d

THE DOOFUS

Most of the insults you throw at him are over his head, but he's mean and gets a kick out of giving you wedgies. He laughs when the other bullies pick on you and likes to join in whenever he can. Attack his intelligence to send him packing! (But try to use small words so he'll understand.)

YOU'RE SO DUMB
YOU THOUGHT
THE DARK MARK
WAS IN YOUR
UNDERWEAR.

WARNING

If your bully has a Dark Mark, run in the other direction and never look back!

YOU'RE A BEAST,
BUT THERE'S
NOTHING
FANTASTIC
ABOUT YOU.

EITHER SOMEONE
DROPPED A
DUNGBOMB OR
YOU'RE STANDING
TOO CLOSE TO ME.

STATS/ FACTS

Boggarts hide in dark places because they are afraid of getting picked on.

YOU'RE SO DUMB
THE SORTING HAT
SHOULD'VE SENT
YOU BACK HOME.

ZONKO'S WAS FRESH OUT OF
STINK PELLETS. MIND IF
I THROW YOU INSTEAD?

Famous Wizard Insults

DENISA THE
DELIGHTFUL

Slytherin Denisa the
Delightful's amiable
demeanor, as well as her
popular
anti-muggle-baiting
campaign in the early
1700s, successfully
challenged negative
stereotypes about Slytherin
House until Voldemort
came along.

WHAT'S THAT
IN YOUR TEA
LEAVES? PLEASE
SAY THE GRIM!

THE BEST
THING ABOUT
APPARATING?
BEING ABLE TO
DISAPPEAR WHEN
YOU SHOW UP.

YOU'RE LIKE BERTIE BOTT'S
EVERY FLAVOR BEANS
BECAUSE YOU LOOK LIKE
VOMIT AND REMIND ME
OF BOOGERS.

THE UNOFFICIAL HARRY POTTER INSULTS HANDBOOK

R.A.T.s POP QUIZ

(REAL-LIFE APPLICATION TEST)

TEST 3: FORESEEING A BULLY-FREE FUTURE

Let's be honest, Divination has never been your best subject. You're talented in Transfiguration and you're a prodigy in Potions, but you can't seem to wrap your head around tea leaves and crystal balls. Plus, you've always been a bit on the clumsy side.

As you bend to retrieve your copy of "Unfogging The Future" from your bag during class, you knock your teacup to the floor, spilling the scalding liquid onto your foot and causing the table of girls beside you to collapse into giggles.

One of the girls — the one who's been tormenting you since you were a lowly first-year — leans over and whispers waspishly, "You know, when I look into my tea leaves, I see you failing this class and everyone realizing you're a squib."

That familiar pricking begins behind your eyes, but you force the tears back and without even a whisper of Accio, you summon all your courage and...

a. Take your seat and hope Professor Trelawney predicts the bully's death next.

b. Ask Professor McGonagall if you can switch to second-period Muggle Studies.

c. Say "What's that in your tea leaves? Please say the Grim!"

d. Grab the nearest crystal ball and throw it at her.

Correct Answer: c

THE PUNKS

These tough guys hide behind the Quidditch field bleachers just waiting to punch your face in. They think they're tough with their nose rings and torn robes, but it's just an act to cover up their own insecurities. A well-delivered insult will get them off your back for good.

I WISH THE INVISIBILITY CLOAK WOULD MAKE YOU DISAPPEAR FOREVER.

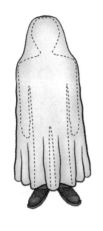

I'VE HAD FIVE BUTTERBEERS AND YOU'RE STILL ANNOYING.

YOUR FACE BROKE COLIN CREEVEY'S CAMERA.

famous WIZARD Insults

MERLIN

A bully once dyed Merlin's beard bright purple while he slept. When he later walked outside, people exclaimed, "Merlin's beard!" and that's how the expression originated.

I BET IF YOU LOOKED A BASILISK IN THE EYE, IT WOULD DIE.

I GOT A
PENSIEVE
SO I COULD
REMEMBER A
TIME I DIDN'T
KNOW YOU.

I'VE HAD BETTER CONVERSATIONS
WITH PORTRAITS.

PRACTICAL JOKE

*Send Nearly Headless Nick
to get your bully for the
Headless Hunt in the
middle of the night.*

YOU'D LOOK
BETTER IF YOU
JOINED THE
HEADLESS HUNT.

I'VE MET SQUIBS
WITH MORE TALENT.

DID YOU KNOW?

No one messed with squib
Arabella Figg because
she was quick with
insults.

WELL, I GUESS MY
FLESH-EATING SLUG
REPELLANT
DOESN'T WORK.

THERE ARE 700 POSSIBLE FOULS
IN A QUIDDITCH GAME. YOUR
ATTENDANCE IS ONE OF THEM.

EVERY TIME I SEE
YOU, I WANT TO DRINK
FORGETFULNESS POTION.

GO SPLINCH
YOURSELF.

IF I HAD A
TIME-TURNER,
I'D GO BACK TO
BEFORE YOU
EXISTED.

I WISH SOMEONE
WOULD OBLIVIATE
MY MEMORY
OF YOU.

PRACTICAL JOKE

*Draw a scar on your bully's
head while he sleeps and
leave a note saying
Voldemort is coming
for him.*

THE ONLY
ACCESSORY THAT
COULD SAVE
THAT OUTFIT IS
AN INVISIBILITY
CLOAK.

THE SNOB

He insults you, your family and your pet Pygmy Puff — nothing is sacred! Plus, he always brags about his expensive clothes while laughing at your outfits with his cronies. Use witty insults against this guy to damage his pride.

YOU'RE SO UGLY
YOU COULD GET A
JOB AT GRINGOTTS.

YOU LOOK LIKE
SOMETHING
NEWT SCAMANDER
WOULD CAPTURE
AND STUDY.

DID SOMEONE HIT YOU WITH
AN ENGORGEMENT CHARM?

SLYTHERIN
SHOULD'VE LOCKED
YOU IN THE
CHAMBER
OF SECRETS.

STATS/
FACTS

Ilker Bashir got so tired of being tripped in the hallways of Hogwarts that he invented the first magic carpet so he could ride it to class.

THE BOUNCER

This bully's favorite pastime is sitting on your chest and making you hit yourself, and she's even been known to flick newt eyes at you. She's slow but strong, so hurl those insults fast and don't let her catch you or you'll get a swirlie.

YOU SHOULD TRY
A LITTLE REPARO ON YOUR FACE.

IF YOU WERE
A HOUSE-ELF,
YOU'D HAVE
NO PROBLEM
GETTING
CLOTHES.

PRACTICAL JOKE

Sprinkle some Wartcap
Powder into the bully's bed,
but be careful not
to touch it!

YOU'RE
WORSE THAN
A DURSLEY.

NOT EVEN HERMIONE CAN FIGURE
OUT WHY YOU'RE SO THICK.

THERE'S A TROLL HERE TO SEE YOU. HE WANTS HIS SMELL BACK.

DID YOU KNOW?

Trolls smell like boiled cabbage and week-old socks.

THERE SHOULD BE AN ENTIRE WARD AT ST. MUNGO'S DEDICATED TO WHATEVER'S WRONG WITH YOU.

NOT EVEN THE HUFFLEPUFFS WANT YOU.

STATS/ FACTS

Hungarian Horntails are the biggest bullies at dragon school.

WHEN YOU OPENED THE GOLDEN EGG IT SANG, *WHAT'S THAT SMELL SO AWFULLY BAD? GO TAKE A BATH, YOU WARTY LAD!*

THE FRENEMY

This girl acts like your friend in Charms class, but in reality, she's not so charming — the second you walk away, she starts throwing shade! She's incredibly vain, so insult her beauty to get this two-faced witch off your back.

WARNING
Spattergroit is highly contagious, so stay away from anyone with this illness unless you want purple pustules.

EVEN DOBBY WOULDN'T TOUCH YOUR SOCKS.

YOU MAKE ARGUS FILCH LOOK LIKE A BEAUTY QUEEN.

DO YOU HAVE SPATTERGROIT OR DO YOU ALWAYS LOOK LIKE THAT?

THE ROOM OF REQUIREMENT WOULD JUST SUPPLY YOU WITH A PAPER BAG.

DID YOU KNOW?
The Room of Requirement is a nice, quiet place to practice your comebacks.

TRICKS AND TREATS FOR MAGICAL BULLIES

Just as Harry and his friends banded together and formed Dumbledore's Army to fight against evil, so can you!

Now that you're a master of the comeback, spread your knowledge to other bullied witches and wizards. Sharing what you've learned will not only help others and lead to new friendships, but it'll also send those bullies a powerful message: You've got both confidence and a supportive squad, so those bullies no longer have any power over you.

There are numerous benefits to forming your own version of Dumbledore's Army, but the best by far will be the friends and alliances you'll make. After all, isn't that what Dumbledore would do?

ACCIO ARMY!

W.W.D.D.

What would Dumbledore do? Offer help to those who need it at Hogwarts.

INSULTS TO MAKE ALL MAGICAL BULLIES CRY

EVERY TIME I GET CLOSE TO A DEMENTOR, I'M FORCED TO RELIVE OUR EVERY ENCOUNTER.

IF QUIRRELL HAD BEEN CURSING YOU, NO ONE WOULD'VE INTERRUPTED HIS CONCENTRATION.

WHAT DID YOU SAY?
I'M SORRY. I DON'T SPEAK TROLL.

PEOPLE CALL YOU THE BASILISK BECAUSE YOUR LOOKS COULD KILL.

THE WIZARD WHO LIVED

You've read up on proper comeback delivery, learned the tricks of the trade and committed 101 magical insults to memory*. You're well aware of the magical bullying threats out there and have armed yourself accordingly. You've even faced down a bully in Hogsmeade, told off a tormentor on the Quidditch field and informed that fortune-telling troublemaker that she won't be picking on you in the near future.

After observing your progress, the Wizarding Examinations Authority has decided to award you full marks on your R.A.T.s.

CONGRATULATIONS!

You're now ready to face any bully** that comes your way — magical or not. Now go out there and live a bully-free life, little wizard!

*Or you've at least read them.

**But just in case things ever get out of hand, it's best to have a few jinxes up your sleeve. We recommend the Bat-Bogey Hex. It's just gross.

CONJURE UP YOUR OWN INSULTS

Did you think of some great insults that weren't included in this book? Write them down here! Crushing comebacks should be infinite, so come up with as many as your magical heart desires.

_____

_____

_____

_____

_____

_____

_____

_____

_____

_____

_____

MISCHIEF MANAGED.

THE UNOFFICIAL HARRY POTTER INSULTS HANDBOOK

ABOUT THE MISCHIEF MAKERS

Laura J. Moss, a Gryffindor who played Chaser for her house Quidditch team, is an author, a journalist and the co-founder of the Webby-nominated website, AdventureCats.org. Her book "Adventure Cats" is a bestseller, and her homemade Pumpkin Pasties are solidly mediocre. She enjoys hiking, playing with her rescue kitties and writing young-adult novels. Follow her on Twitter and Instagram (@laurajmoss) or visit her online at www.laurajmoss.com.

Birdy Jones, a Ravenclaw who represented her house in the Triwizard Tournament, writes picture books for kids. Author of "Mister Cool" and "Blossom Plays Possum (Because She's Shy)," Birdy loves writing stories that will inspire children to be their own unique selves. She also enjoys tricking her friends into eating the gross flavors of Bertie Bott's Every Flavor Beans. Follow her on Facebook (@birdyjonesstories) and Twitter (@birdy_jones) or visit her website at www.birdyjones.com.

Sterling Martin, a Hufflepuff best known at Hogwarts for getting stuck in the Room of Requirement for a month as a third-year, is a graphic designer, illustrator and writer. He's authored two web comics, "Oranges Are Funny!" and "Fleas on Flick." He enjoys drawing, hanging out with his buddies drinking butterbeer and laughing at a good Weasleys' Wizarding Wheezes' magical prank. You can visit his portfolio to see his work at www.sterlingmartin.design or follow him on Instagram at (@sterfest).

Made in the USA
Middletown, DE
04 December 2018